HAVE YOU HAD YOUR FRUIT TODAY?

HAVE YOU HAD YOUR FRUIT TODAY?

DEVOTIONAL
Nine Fruit of the Spirit

D'Zine By El'laine
Fruit of the Spirit

Brenda T. Vaughn

Copyright

Contents

HAVE YOU HAD YOUR FRUIT TODAY?

Introduction

For years, I felt I wasn't a loving person. My mother passed away when I was four years old, and I have always missed that love from her. I didn't always respond as I should have to others. I dedicate this book to my mother. As a child, one day, I was told, "You can never love a child like you love your own." As a result of the void in my life, I felt I didn't know how to love.

In my spirit, I believe it doesn't matter what people have said about you. It doesn't matter if your mother or father left you years ago. Nothing on this earth can ever hurt or destroy you because of your fruit. God has always confirmed his word in my life over and over. One of his confirmations was to make me aware that I do know how to love. He continues to send messages to me to make me love more deeply.

When I began studying the nine fruit of the Spirit and what God says about how we should carry ourselves, they taught me that I'm strong in Christ. Yes, things will come, but they can't stay because of the light of Christ. Where the light of Christ is, darkness can't remain. Walk in the Light, in the nine fruit of the Spirit.

"But the fruit of the Spirit is love, joy, peace, patience, kindness, goodness, faithfulness, gentleness, and self-control. Those who belong to Christ Jesus have crucified the flesh with its passions and desires" (Galatians 5:22-23 ESV).

As you read and study the nine fruit of the Spirit, each one has space where you can create your prayer and write down your thoughts that God brings to your heart. Always know that God is a healer, and He will bring us into that place of wholeness so that we can walk in the nine fruit of the Spirit. As you learn about them, you will also learn about nine fresh fruit connected to each one of the fruit of the Spirit and how they relate.

Love

Cherries are a reminder of love.

When I think of the cherry, I am reminded of its distinct color, crimson. This is a deep purplish-red color, which brings to mind our blood that flows on the inside. My mind then automatically goes to the redemption of God and the blood that was shed on the cross from His Son Jesus.

Love, life, rebirth, spiritual and mental growth are all attributes that come to mind when I ponder about the cherry.

When I was completing this study, I got the revelation that God truly loves us and wants the best for us. He is calling for reproduction in our lives from the I was into the I am. This is where we need to look at death, of letting the old things in our lives go. He tells us that the old things will pass away (will die). Behold, there will be some new things that will come (being rebirthed), so when we hear the word death or things dying, look at it as a rebirth in our lives, in the mental and spiritual realm.

When I think about rebirth, my mind goes back to the following verse, being that new person every morning, having that new beginning, to start over again.

"Therefore, if anyone is in Christ, he is a new creation. The old has passed away; behold, the new has come" (2 Corinthians 5:17 ESV).

God is a loving God. He gives us peace when we need it. He has shown us his love each and every day of our lives, and God's love for us never changes, regardless of our circumstances.

Cherries 🍒 are the Fruit for Love
Create your own Prayer

_____

_____

_____

_____

_____

_____

_____

_____

_____

_____

_____

_____

_____

_____

_____

_____

_____

Cherries

"We love because he first loved us."
(1 John 4:19 ESV)
Meditate on the Word

_____

_____

_____

_____

_____

_____

_____

_____

_____

_____

_____

_____

_____

_____

_____

_____

_____

_____

Love

God is love. I thank him for the gift of love, even when I fall short in my life. God is still there, and he loves me.

Cherries 🍒 are a reminder of love.
We think about love when we think about cherries!
🍒
Create your own Prayer

_____

_____

_____

_____

_____

_____

_____

_____

_____

_____

_____

Cherries

"Dear friends, if God loved us this way, we also ought to love each other" (1John 4:11 CEB).

Meditate on the Word

_____

_____

_____

_____

_____

_____

_____

_____

_____

_____

_____

_____

_____

_____

_____

Love
Thank you for being a loving Father,
for protecting me from the enemies, and for
shielding me from hurt and harm. Most of all,
thank you for the blood of Jesus.

Cherries 🍒 are a reminder of love.

Love is like cherries.

🍒

Create your own Prayer

_____

_____

_____

_____

_____

_____

_____

_____

_____

Cherries

"By this it is evident who are the children of God, and who are the children of the devil: whoever does not practice righteousness is not of God, nor is the one who does not love his brother. For this is the message that you have heard from the beginning, that we should love one another" (1 John 3:10-11 ESV).

Meditate on the Word

_____

_____

_____

_____

_____

_____

_____

_____

_____

Joy

When I reflect on this next fruit of the Spirit, joy, I am reminded of grapes.

In the Bible, grapes symbolize blessings, goodness, good things, and prosperity. God's word tells us that His blessings make us rich, and it adds no sorrow to it. He makes us prosperous in all of our ways.

Reference scripture
"The blessing of the Lord makes rich, and he adds no sorrow with it" (Proverbs 10:22 ESV).

Stand still and see the salvation of God in your life.

Grapes

God gave His only Son that I may have joy in my life. As I've traveled down so many pathways, He has put joy down within me because Jesus paved the way. Now, I can always have that joy.

Grapes are the fruit for joy.
Joy is like grapes.

Create your own Prayer

_____

_____

_____

_____

_____

_____

_____

_____

Grapes

"This is the day that the Lord has made; let us rejoice and be glad in it" (Psalms 118:24 ESV).

Meditate on the Word

_____

_____

_____

_____

_____

_____

_____

_____

_____

_____

_____

_____

_____

_____

_____

_____

Grapes

Father, let nothing separate us from your joy because I know that the joy of the Lord is my strength.

Grapes 🍇 are the fruit for joy.
Grapes symbolize joy.

🍇

Create your own Prayer

_____
_____
_____
_____
_____
_____
_____
_____
_____
_____
_____
_____

Grapes

"I have rejoiced in the way of thy testimonies,
as much as in all riches" (Psalms 119:14 KJV).

Meditate on the Word

_____

_____

_____

_____

_____

_____

_____

_____

_____

_____

_____

_____

_____

_____

_____

_____

Joy

God, I thank you for allowing me to be in your presence that is filled with joy. I have the privilege to have been given peace and walk in the fullness of joy. Even when everything around me is turning upside down, there is still joy in you.

Grapes 🍇 are the fruit for joy.
Joy is like grapes.
🍇
Create your own Prayer

_____
_____
_____
_____
_____
_____
_____
_____
_____

Grapes

Rejoicing in hope; patient in tribulation; continuing instant in prayer" (Roman 12:12 KJV).

Meditate on the Word

_____

_____

_____

_____

_____

_____

_____

_____

_____

_____

_____

_____

_____

_____

_____

_____

Peace

The fruit that represents peace is the apple. Sitting down meditating brings me to that quiet place, reflecting on the knowledge, wisdom, and joy of the Lord.

Our Father left his peace with us, not the peace of this world. The peace that the Father left here for me is calming. He doesn't desire for me to be anxious for anything.

The apple symbolizes peace.

Peace is like an Apple

Create your own Prayer

_____

_____

_____

Peace

"Keep me as the apple of your eye; hide me in the shadow of your wings" (Psalm 17:8 ESV).

Meditate on the Word

_____

_____

_____

_____

_____

_____

_____

_____

_____

_____

_____

_____

_____

_____

_____

Peace

Our Father left his peace with us, not the peace of this world. The peace that the Father left here for me is calming. He doesn't desire for me to be anxious for anything.

God, you have given me the prescription for peace of mind. Resting in your peace is a strong foundation in having compassion for others.

Biblical Reference: "When a man's ways please the Lord, he makes even his enemies to be at peace with him" (Proverbs 16:7 ESV).

The apple 🍎 symbolizes peace.
Peace is like an apple.

🍎

Create your own Prayer

_____

_____

_____

_____

_____

_____

_____

_____

_____

_____

_____

_____

_____

_____

_____

_____

_____

_____

Apple

O Lord, you will ordain peace for us, for you have indeed done for us all our works" (Isaiah 26:12 ESV).

Meditate on the Word

_____

_____

_____

_____

_____

_____

_____

_____

_____

_____

_____

_____

_____

_____

_____

_____

Peace

Thank you for leaving your peace with us, that peace that protects us from the spirit of depression. Thank you for keeping me when I'm feeling weak.

Lord, thank you for carrying my burdens. Thank you for your presence. Thank you for leaving your peace during troubled times. In the midst of confusion, you release all of my burdens.

"You keep him in perfect peace whose mind is stayed on you because he trusts in you" (Isaiah 26:3 ESV).

The apple symbolizes peace.
Peace is like an Apple.

Create your own Prayer

_____

_____

_____

_____

_____

_____

_____

_____

_____

_____

_____

_____

_____

_____

_____

_____

Apple

Peace I leave with you; my peace I give to you. Not as the world gives do I give to you. Let not your hearts be troubled, neither let them be afraid" (John 14: 27 ESV).

Meditate on the Word

_____

_____

_____

_____

_____

_____

_____

_____

_____

_____

_____

_____

_____

_____

_____

Patience

The fruit that symbolizes patience is the pear. When reflecting on the pear, it brings to my mind prosperity, grace, wisdom, and good health.

The grace of God rains down on me each and every day and allows me to be patient. He has placed that inner peace down on the inside, and this is also a sign of prosperity because he keeps me and protects me from getting what the enemy tries to send up against me. What a blessing it is to walk in God's prosperity in all areas of our lives.

Biblical Reference:

"And thus shall ye say to him that liveth in prosperity, Peace be both to thee, and peace be to thine house, and peace be unto all that thou hast" (I Samuel 25:6 KJV).

Patience

The Lord has given us the patience to endure all things at all times. I am always in his presence.

The pear 🍐 symbolizes patience.
Patience is like a pear.

🍐

Create your own Prayer

_____

_____

_____

_____

_____

_____

_____

_____

Pear

God says, "Be still and know that I am God. I will be praised in all the nations; I will be praised throughout the earth" (Psalms 46:10 NCV).

Meditate on the Word

_____

_____

_____

_____

_____

_____

_____

_____

_____

_____

_____

_____

_____

_____

Patience

Lord, thank you for patience in my daily living, It will shine a brighter light on life's problems.

The pear 🍐 is the fruit for patience.

Patience is like a pear.

🍐

Create your own Prayer

_____

_____

_____

_____

_____

_____

_____

_____

_____

_____

_____

Pear

"Be still before the Lord and wait patiently for him; fret not yourself over the one who prospers in his way, over the man who carries out evil devices" (Psalms 37:7 ESV).

Meditate on the Word

_____

_____

_____

_____

_____

_____

_____

_____

_____

_____

_____

_____

Patience

Thank you, Father, for allowing us to rest in your patience. Your patience plays a very important part in my life. I must learn to be more patient in my relationships with others. Having patience allows me to let go and allows you to work in and through me.

The pear 🍐 is the fruit for patience.

Patience is like a pear.

🍐

Create your own Prayer

_____

_____

_____

_____

_____

_____

_____

_____

_____

_____

Pear

"Be patient, therefore, brothers, until the coming of the Lord. See how the farmer waits for the precious fruit of the earth, being patient about it until it receives the early and the late rains. You also be patient. Establish your hearts, for the coming of the Lord is at hand" (James 5: 7-8 ESV).

Meditate on the Word

_____

_____

_____

_____

_____

_____

_____

_____

_____

_____

_____

Kindness

The fruit that represents kindness is pineapple. My thoughts and meaning for the pineapple are hospitality of families, true friendship, being refreshed, and renewed.

I'm reminded of my story and what I shared in my book *Walking Out of the I was Into the I Am*. I told my life story of how I loved to entertain all the time. I always wanted to host others. When I look at my life today, I still love to host and entertain people. God didn't take that away from me. He added more to me as a believer and leader. I just host differently, in a spiritual way, having an open heart to help others the way Christ has helped and cared for others.

God loves families. God's hospitality started with me and my family first. Now, I'm able to reach out and bring my true friends to the table so that they will be refreshed in their lives.

Biblical Reference:

"Above all, keep loving one another earnestly, since love covers a multitude of sins. Show hospitality to one another without grumbling" (1 Peter 4:8-9 ESV).

Kindness

Father, thank you for allowing me to operate in your kindness. You have lifted us out of darkness and into your marvelous light. We rest in your loving-kindness, and I can show kindness to others.

The pineapple is the fruit for kindness.

When we meditate on the word kindness, we learn it's just nice to be kind to one another. The Bible tells us to treat others the way we want to be treated.

"Treat people in the same way that you want them to treat you" (Luke 6:31 CEB).

The pineapple is like kindness.

Create your own Prayer

_____

_____

_____

_____

_____

_____

_____

_____

Pineapple

"He has been very kind and patient, waiting for you to change, but you think nothing of his kindness. Perhaps you do not understand that God is kind to you so you will change your hearts and lives" (Romans 2:4 NCV).

Meditate on the Word

_____

_____

_____

_____

_____

_____

_____

_____

_____

_____

_____

_____

_____

_____

_____

_____

_____

_____

_____

_____

_____

_____

Kindness

God, you want me to be kind and show your love. Your word teaches me that your kindness is better than anything else.

The pineapple 🍍 is what symbolizes kindness. Kindness is like the pineapple.

🍍

Create your own Prayer

_____

_____

_____

_____

_____

_____

_____

_____

_____

_____

_____

_____

_____

Pineapple

"For thy loving kindness is better than life: therefore, my lips shall praise thee" (Psalms 63:3 GNV)

Meditate on the Word

_____

_____

_____

_____

_____

_____

_____

_____

_____

_____

_____

_____

_____

_____

_____

_____

Kindness

When I went through the darkest hours of my life and felt down in the dumps, you took those dark days and hours. You turned those days into rivers of water. Now, I'm gleaned as a jewel, in the kindness of your love.

The pineapple 🍍 is the fruit for kindness.

Kindness is like a pineapple.
🍍
Create your own Prayer

_____

_____

_____

_____

_____

_____

_____

_____

_____

_____

Pineapple

"He has been very kind and patient, waiting for you to change, but you think nothing of his kindness. Perhaps you do not understand that God is kind to you so you will change your hearts and lives" (Romans 2:4 NCV).

Meditate on the Word

_____

_____

_____

_____

_____

_____

_____

_____

_____

_____

_____

_____

Goodness

The fruit for goodness is the peach.

The peach reminds me of springtime, the newness of life, charm, softness, peace, and purity.

God has given His Son Jesus for us. He brings us that spring water in our lives. When I'm thirsty for other things, He is always there speaking in my life with that soft voice, bringing me that peace that I need to get me to the next level. When I walk with God, I'm walking in His purity as His bride.

Once we come to Christ, we walk in the peace and the purity of God.

Biblical Reference:
"Jesus said to him, "I am the way, and the truth, and the life. No one comes to the Father except through me" (John 14:6 ESV).

Goodness

God, I thank you for your goodness. When I leave and return home each day, your goodness surrounds me. You allow me to have my physical health and strength. That's goodness. As a gentle breeze on a hot day, your goodness is refreshing. When I lay down each day, and when I rise in the morning, there is your goodness. When we hear the birds singing, there is your goodness.

The peach ♡ is the fruit that represents goodness.

Goodness is like peaches.

Create your own Prayer

_____

_____

_____

_____

_____

_____

_____

_____

_____

_____

_____

_____

_____

_____

_____

_____

_____

_____

Peaches

"And God can give you more blessings than you need. Then you will always have plenty of everything—enough to give to every good work" (2 Corinthians 9:8 NCV).

Meditate on the Word

_____

_____

_____

_____

_____

_____

_____

_____

_____

_____

_____

_____

_____

_____

Goodness

God, I thank you for life and a chance to get it right.

The peach 🍑 is the fruit for goodness.

Goodness is like peaches.

🍑

Create your own Prayer

_____

_____

_____

_____

_____

_____

_____

_____

_____

_____

_____

_____

_____

_____

Peaches

"For everything created by God is good, and nothing is to be rejected if it is received with thanksgiving" (1 Timothy 4:4 ESV).

Meditate on the Word

_____

_____

_____

_____

_____

_____

_____

_____

_____

_____

_____

_____

_____

_____

_____

_____

Goodness

In the midst of all of the trails, troubles, and temptations, you are everlasting.

The peach 🍑 is the fruit for goodness.

Goodness is like peaches.

🍑

Create your own Prayer

_____

_____

_____

_____

_____

_____

_____

_____

_____

_____

_____

_____

_____

Peaches

"Surely goodness and mercy shall follow me all the days of my life, and I shall dwell in the house of the Lord forever" (Psalms 23:6 ESV).

Meditate on the Word

_____

_____

_____

_____

_____

_____

_____

_____

_____

_____

_____

_____

_____

_____

Faithfulness

The fruit that I admonished for faithfulness is oranges. When I look at the color of the orange, it takes my mind to the abundance of wealth, joy, success and eternal life.

In the book of Matthew, it tells us that all our success, joy, wealth, and eternal life are stored up in heaven and not on earth.

Biblical Reference:
"Lay not up for yourselves treasures upon the earth, where moth and rust consume, and where thieves break through and steal: but lay up for yourselves treasures in heaven, where neither moth nor rust

doth consume, and where thieves do not break through nor steal" (Matthew 6:19-20 ASV).

God has given us eternal life to live forever and to walk in wealth. What a beautiful thing. He has allowed us to shine and has shown us off as his children.

Faithfulness

God, I thank you for your faithfulness. Thank you for awaking me every morning, allowing me to dress myself, to put food on the table, having a warm place to lay my head, allowing me to have people in our lives and the love that they have shown. For that, I say thank you for being faithful.

The orange 🍊 is the fruit for faithfulness.
Faithfulness is like an orange.

🍊

Create your own Prayer

_____

_____

_____

_____

_____

_____

_____

_____

_____

_____

Orange

"But you, O Lord, are a God merciful and gracious, slow to anger and abounding in steadfast love and faithfulness" (Psalms 86:15 ESV).

Meditate on the Word

_____

_____

_____

_____

_____

_____

_____

_____

_____

_____

_____

_____

_____

_____

Faithfulness

Father, help us to be faithful over your money, over your houses, over your land, over your people, over the jobs you have given us, over your cars, over your marriages, and over your relationships.

Father, you have been faithful to me;
you have been faithful in all things.

The orange 🍊 is the fruit like faithfulness.

Faithfulness is like the oranges.
🍊
Create your own Prayer

_____

_____

_____

_____

_____

_____

_____

Orange

"Therefore know [without any doubt] and understand that the LORD your God, He is God, the faithful God, who is keeping His covenant and His [steadfast] lovingkindness to a thousand generations with those who love Him and keep His commandments" (Deuteronomy 7:9 AMP).

Meditate on the Word

_____

_____

_____

_____

_____

_____

_____

_____

_____

_____

_____

Faithfulness

God, your word says, "If I'm faithful over a few things, you will make me ruler over many. God, sometimes we think we are faithful over the things you have given us. When we are not faithful, help us not to take your blessings for granted. You were faithful on calvary; you paid the price for all of our sin.

The orange 🍊 is the fruit for faithfulness.

Faithfulness is like the orange.

🍊

Create your own Prayer

_____

_____

_____

_____

_____

_____

_____

_____

Faithfulness is like oranges.

Orange

"His master said to him, 'Well done, good and faithful servant. You have been faithful and trustworthy over a little, I will put you in charge of many things; share in the joy of your master" (Matthew 25:23 AMP).

Meditate on the Word

_____

_____

_____

_____

_____

_____

_____

_____

_____

_____

_____

_____

Gentleness

The fruit for gentleness is the banana. To me, this fruit resembles money and signifies saving, love, and happiness.

"Whoever trusts in his riches will fall, but the righteous will flourish like a green leaf" (Proverbs 11:28 ASV).

From time to time, I hear God wants us to live a certain way. God owns everything, and he wants us to have the best. I believe when God blesses us with things, we are to give these things back to him for His glory and tell Him thank you for the things that he has given us. It's not that he doesn't want us to live without. That is opposite of the way He thinks. God wants us to prosper as our soul prospers.

Gentleness

God is gentle, and he leads us through His Word. He is a gentle spirit, and that spirit is transferred to us.

The banana 🍌 is the fruit that represents gentleness.

Gentleness is like a banana.

🍌

Create your own Prayer

_____

_____

_____

_____

_____

_____

_____

_____

_____

_____

_____

_____

Banana

"But the wisdom from above is first pure [morally and spiritually undefiled], then peace-loving [courteous, considerate], gentle, reasonable [and willing to listen], full of compassion and good fruits. It is unwavering, without [self-righteous] hypocrisy [and self-serving guile]" (James 3:17 AMP).

Meditate on the Word

_____

_____

_____

_____

_____

_____

_____

_____

_____

_____

_____

_____

Gentleness

Father, thank you for your gentleness in my heart, which allows me to be that peacemaker as I grow.

The banana 🍌 is like fruit for gentleness.

Gentleness is like a banana.

🍌

Create your own Prayer

_____

_____

_____

_____

_____

_____

_____

_____

_____

_____

_____

_____

Banana

"A soft and gentle and thoughtful answer turns away wrath, But harsh and painful and careless words stir up anger" (Proverbs 15:1 AMP).

Meditate on the Word

_____

_____

_____

_____

_____

_____

_____

_____

_____

_____

_____

_____

_____

_____

_____

Gentleness

Father, I thank you that when I'm waking in gentleness, you help me know I'm not weak, but I'm being made strong. Being meek helps me deal with my attitude towards others.

The banana 🍌 is the fruit for gentleness.

Gentleness is like a banana.

🍌

Create your own Prayer

_____

_____

_____

_____

_____

_____

_____

_____

_____

_____

Banana

"Be kind to one another, tenderhearted, forgiving one another, as God in Christ forgave you" (Ephesians 4:32 ESV).

Medicate on the Word

_____

_____

_____

_____

_____

_____

_____

_____

_____

_____

_____

_____

_____

_____

_____

_____

_____

Self -Control

This fruit of the spirit is very important. Out of all the fruit, it takes self-control to be able to operate in the other eight. When I think of watermelon, it symbolizes love, work, welfare And desires.

"This is how everyone will know that you are my disciples, when you love each other" (John 13:35 CEB).

As we walk through this life, having self-control is being able to control our feelings and emotions. We will always be concerned about our well-being as we walk in love and have the desire to move forward and never give up.

Father, thank you for giving us awareness and self-control that is pleasing to you in all areas of our lives. You don't desire that we mistreat family. You desire that we show respect and love to others and ourselves.

The watermelon 🍉 symbolizes self-control.

Self-Control is like a watermelon.

🍉

Create your own Prayer

_____

_____

_____

_____

_____

_____

_____

_____

_____

_____

Watermelon

"No temptation has overtaken you that is not common to man. God is faithful, and he will not let you be tempted beyond your ability, but with the temptation he will also provide the way of escape, that you may be able to endure it" (1 Corinthians 10:13 ESV).

Meditate

_____

_____

_____

_____

_____

_____

_____

_____

_____

_____

_____

_____

_____

_____

Self-Control

Lord, it takes self-control to have love, joy, peace, patience, kindness, goodness, faithfulness, and gentleness. It takes self-control to have self-control.

The nine Fruit of the Spirit.

The watermelon is the fruit for self-control.

Self-Control is like a watermelon.

Create your own Prayer

_____

_____

_____

_____

_____

_____

_____

_____

_____

_____

Watermelon

"For we do not wrestle against flesh and blood, but against the rulers, against the authorities, against the cosmic powers over this present darkness, against the spiritual forces of evil in the heavenly places" (Ephesians 6:12 ESV).

Meditate on the Word

_____

_____

_____

_____

_____

_____

_____

_____

_____

_____

_____

_____

_____

Self-Control

Father, self-control is something that I need in my life. I need self-control with my time, in my spending, to keep me from overeating, when to speak, and when to be silent. Father, help me to be a good steward in your sight as I practice self-control.

The watermelon 🍉 is the fruit for self-control.

Self-Control is like a watermelon.

🍉

Create your own Prayer

_____

_____

_____

_____

_____

_____

_____

_____

_____

Watermelon

"Do not be conformed to this world, but be transformed by the renewal of your mind, that by testing you may discern what is the will of God, what is good and acceptable and perfect" (Romans 12:2 ESV).

Meditate on the Word

_____

_____

_____

_____

_____

_____

_____

_____

_____

_____

_____

_____

_____

About the Author

B renda T. Vaughn is a pastor in Atlanta, GA. God has blessed her to run an outreach center, The Heart of God International Outreach Ministries.

Brenda owns the company D'zine by El'laine
Check out some of her items below:
12 different sayings 3-candles (unscented)
Large candles Fruit of the Spirit (unscented)
9 (scented) candles for each Fruit of the Spirit
Nine different Fruit of the Spirit body soap
Fruit of the Spirit mousepads
Fruit of the Spirit note pads
Box of (3) Fruit of the Spirit greeting cards
(Love, Joy, and Peace)
Box of (9) Fruit of The Spirit Greeting Cards
(Love Joy, Peace, Patience, Kindness

Goodness, Faithfulness, Gentleness, and Self-Control)

9 Fruit of the Spirit Scented Anointed Body Oil

Other products are coming soon.

Contact Brenda T. Vaughn

For Booking Contact Brenda T. Vaughn
brendavaughn6@gmail.com

AVAILABLE TITLES

IF YOU ENJOYED THIS BOOK, HERE ARE OTHER TITLES
BRENDA T. VAUGHN
BOOK AVAILABLE ON AMAZON:
2020

Walking Out of the I was into the I Am (Book)

Coming Soon

Everyday Prayer Devotional

You Are A Priceless Diamond 30 Days Inspirational Devotional Workbook Volume (1)

You Are A Priceless Diamond 30 Days Inspirational Devotional Workbook Volume (2)

www.ingramcontent.com/pod-product-compliance
Lightning Source LLC
Chambersburg PA
CBHW070204060426
42445CB00032B/1212